Helen Marlais'

Succeeding at the Piano®

A Method for Everyone

ISBN-13: 978-1-56939-847-0

Production: Frank J. Hackinson
Production Coordinators: Joyce Loke, Satish Bhakta, and Philip Groeber
Editors: Joyce Loke, Edwin McLean, Peggy Gallagher, and
 Nancy Bona-Baker
Art Direction: Sandy Brandvold and Andi Whitmer –
 in collaboration with Helen Marlais
Cover and Interior Illustrations: ©2010 Susan Hellard/Arena
Cover and Interior Illustration Concepts: Helen Marlais
Engraving: Tempo Music Press, Inc.
Printer: Tempo Music Press, Inc.

Grade 1 - Table of Contents

FJH2058

For the Student

Throughout this book you will do many different activities such as:

Writing:

After you write the answers, you can play them on the piano.

Rhythm:

Just as this boy and girl walk in rhythm together, you will feel the steady beat in every rhythm activity!

Time to Compose:

Your very own compositions can be just as important as the pieces you learn.

Ear Training:

Learn notes and patterns in music by using your ears carefully.

Follow the Leader:

Use your ears to hear *rhythmic* patterns.

Parrot Play:

Use your ears to hear *musical* patterns.

Review of Preparatory Level

Help the bald eagle fly back to his big nest by the sea. Circle the wings that are correct. Then draw a line from one correct wing to the next until he is home!

bass clef

full note

half note

repeat sign

bass C

5th up

GAB

3rd (skip) down

F

4th up

tie

slur

treble clef

DEF

Did you know?
Bald Eagles mate for life!

FJH2058

Rhythm

1. Add a time signature to each rhythm pattern below. Draw a line from the rhythm on the left to the rhythm that matches it on the right.

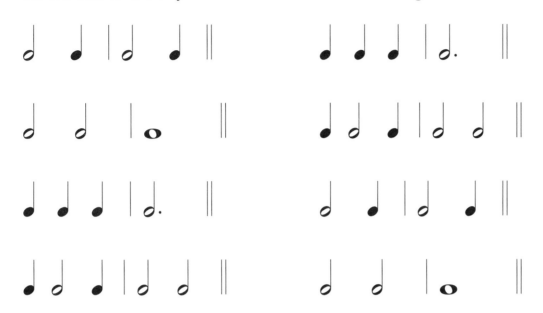

2. Cross out the measures that have too many beats.

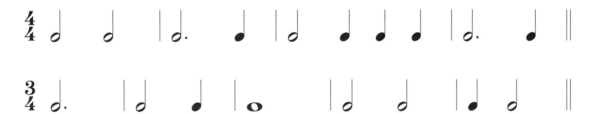

3. Fill in the bar lines for the following rhythms.

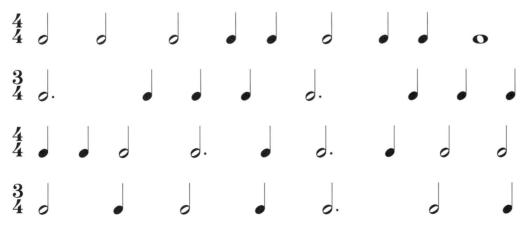

Dynamics

- Draw a line from each dynamic mark on the left to the correct answer on the right.

p   a little less loud than *f*

mp   loud

mf   soft

f   a little louder than *p*

- Write *p*, *mp*, *mf*, or *f* by the picture that matches.

Time to Compose:

- Make up a piece in C Position.
- Decide the time signature.
- Use two dynamic marks using the pictures above.

My title: _____

★ Practice your piece as many times as it takes to completely remember it!

Mr. Cricket

- Fill in the names of the notes to complete the story.

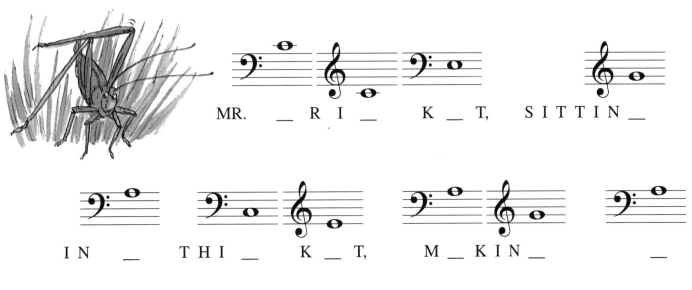

MR. _ R I _ K _ T,   S I T T I N _

I N _ T H I _ K _ T,   M _ K I N _   _

S W _ _ T,   S W _ _ T   S O U N _!

MR. _ R I _ K _ T, IS JUST TH _   T I _ K _ T,

T O H _ _ R   T H _   _ _ S T

M _ L O _ Y   I N T H _   T O W N!

UNIT 2

Interval Review

An **interval** is the distance between two keys on the piano.

- Write "M" for melodic interval, and "H" for harmonic interval.
- Name each interval.

H 3rd

_____

_____

_____

_____

_____

_____

_____

_____

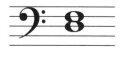

_____

_____

_____

FJH2058

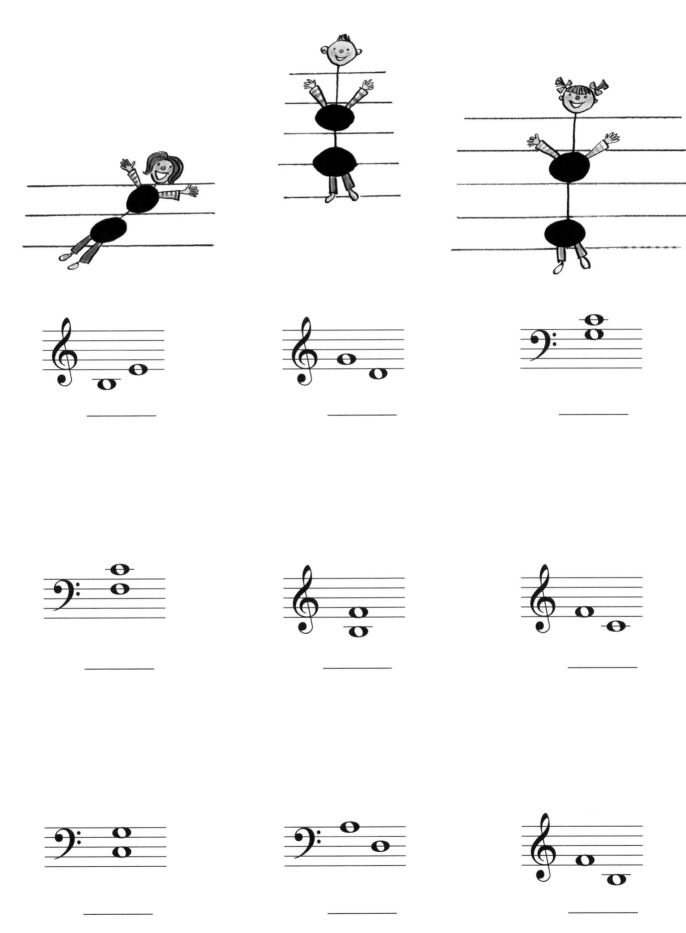

• Now find and play the intervals!

Slurs and Ties

A slur under or over different notes means to play smoothly. The Italian word for playing "smoothly" is *legato*.

A tie connects one note to the very same note. Hold the second note and count both notes.

• Write "S" for slur, and "T" for tie. Then play each example on the piano.

   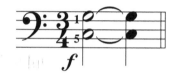

• Draw a slur **over** the notes. Then play the pattern slowly, listening to the *legato* sound. →

• Draw a slur **under** the notes. Then play the pattern slowly, listening to the *legato* sound. →

FJH2058

Time to Compose:

- Make up a melody in the R.H. and write it on the staff.
- Add a title about a hippo!

_____
(my title)

Ear Training:

- Your teacher will play melodic (broken) or harmonic (blocked) intervals. Listen carefully!

- Write "M" for melodic and "H" for harmonic.

1. _____   2. _____   3. _____

4. _____   5. _____   6. _____

For teacher use: (To be played in any order.)

Follow the Leader:

- Listen to your teacher clap a rhythm.
- Can you clap it back?

For teacher use:
(Use any of these rhythms or others you might like!)

A Above Guide Note G

- Below are the notes you know.
- Write the letter names.
- Then find and play them on the piano.

NEW NOTE: A

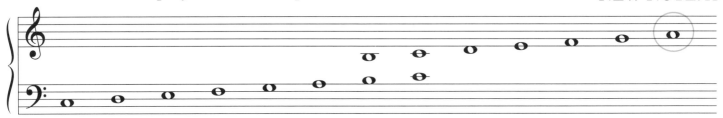

- Follow the bumblebees from one note to the next.
- Write the letter name of each note.
- Then find and play each one on the piano.

FJH2058

Quarter Rest

♩ Quarter note = 1 beat

𝄽 Quarter rest = 1 beat of silence

• Trace these quarter rests 𝄽 𝄽 𝄽 𝄽

Draw 2 rests on your own:

Our Mouse

• Fill in the time signature.
• Write the counting under the notes.
• Clap and count aloud. Whisper the rests.
• Tap and say the words.

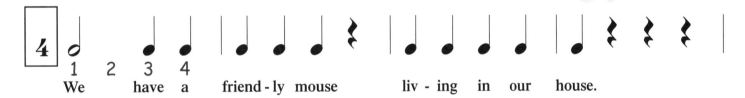

1   2   3   4
We   have   a   friend - ly mouse   liv - ing   in   our   house.

He   likes   to   sniff;   he   likes   to   run.

Some   peo - ple   scream in fright   when they   see   our   mouse.

He   looks and   smiles at them as   he   sits   on   the   couch!

Staccato

Staccato means to play with a short, separated sound.

To play *staccato*, spring quickly from the key, wrist **first**.

- Name the intervals below.
- Circle all of the *staccato* harmonic intervals.
- Then play **all** of the intervals on the piano, listening to the different sounds.

1.

2.

3.

4.

5.

6.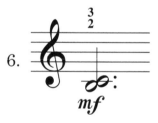

- Write the names of the notes. Play and listen to the difference in sound.
  Staccato and *legato* are opposite!

1.

2.

3.

4.

FJH2058

The Wall of Mirrors

• Draw a line from each mirror to its identical match.

The Sharp Sign ♯

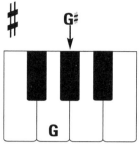
 = G♯

Notice the sharp sign in front of the G note above.

When you see a ♯, play the very next key **higher** (black or white).

1.

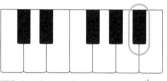

This key is _____ ♯.
Find it and play it!

This key is _____ ♯.
Find it and play it!

2. Write the names of the notes below, then play them.

Circle the correct keys on the keyboard below each staff.

F   F♯

   ___   ___

   ___   ___

3. Add a sharp before each note. The **center** of the ♯ is **always** on the **same** line or space as the note head.

Then write the letter names.

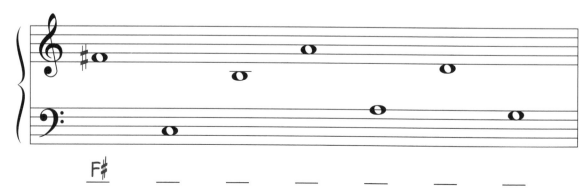

F♯   ___   ___   ___   ___   ___

FJH2058

4. Draw ♯'s in front of the line notes:

Draw ♯'s in front of the space notes:

Then, write in the name of the notes. Play them on the piano.

5. A sharp (♯) lasts through an entire measure. The bar line cancels the ♯.

- Circle the G♯'s.
- Play the notes.

- Circle the F♯'s.
- Play the notes.

6. **Time to Compose:**

- Make up a piece using ♯'s.
- Will your piece be in $\frac{3}{4}$ or $\frac{4}{4}$ time?

My title: _____

Some ideas: in a balloon, taking off in an airplane, a tack on a chair.

The Flat Sign ♭

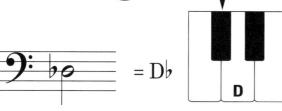

 = D♭

Notice the flat sign in front of the D note above.
When you see a ♭, play the very next key
lower (black or white).

1.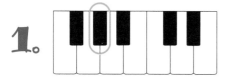

This key is _____ ♭.
Find it and play it!

This key is _____ ♭.
Find it and play it!

2. Write the name of the notes below, then play them.
Circle the correct keys on the keyboard below each staff.

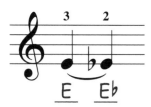
3   2
E   E♭

3   2
___   ___

2   3
___   ___

2   3
___   ___

3. Add a flat before each note. The **center** of the ♭ is **always** on the **same** line or
space as the note head.
Then write the letter names.

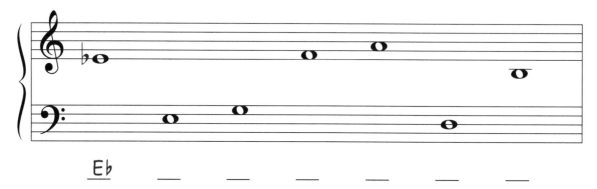

E♭   ___   ___   ___   ___   ___

FJH2058

4. Draw ♭'s in front of the space notes:

Draw ♭'s in front of the line notes:

Then, write in the name of the notes. Play them on the piano.

5. A flat (♭) lasts through an entire measure. The bar line cancels the ♭.

- Circle the D♭'s.
- Play the notes.

- Circle the G♭'s.
- Play the notes.

6. **Time to Compose:**

- Make up a piece using ♭'s.
- Will your piece be in $\frac{3}{4}$ or $\frac{4}{4}$ time?

My title: _____

Some ideas: bike with a flat tire, walking down the steps, landing in an airplane, sledding downhill.

Parrot Play:

Parrots love to repeat what they hear!

- Your teacher will play *Little Bo Peep*.
- Sing it together.
- Can you play the beginning of it **by ear**?

Learn a little of it at a time. Watch and listen carefully.

Little Bo Peep

Traditional

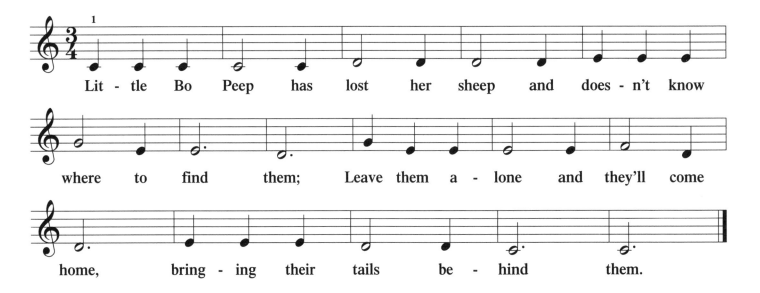

Lit - tle Bo Peep has lost her sheep and does - n't know

where to find them; Leave them a - lone and they'll come

home, bring - ing their tails be - hind them.

- Now play *Little Bo Peep* starting on G.

FJH2058

UNIT 5

G Position

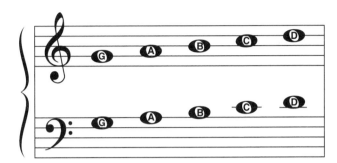

1. Fill in the names of the intervals and the notes.
Then find and play them on the piano in rhythm!

3rd up

G   B

2. Draw the bar lines and add the time signature. Then play the example.

3. Each measure is incomplete. Add one or more notes or rests to complete the measures.
Use any of these notes:

Now play it!

Tempo

Tempo = the speed of a piece.

- Draw a line from each composer to the matching tempo.

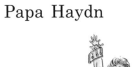

Papa Haydn

Beethoven

adagio (slowly)

andante (walking speed)

moderato (moderate speed)

allegro (happy, spirited)

Mozart

Brahms

Magic Words

- Write the counting under the notes.
- Clap and count aloud (whisper the rests).
- Tap and say the words.

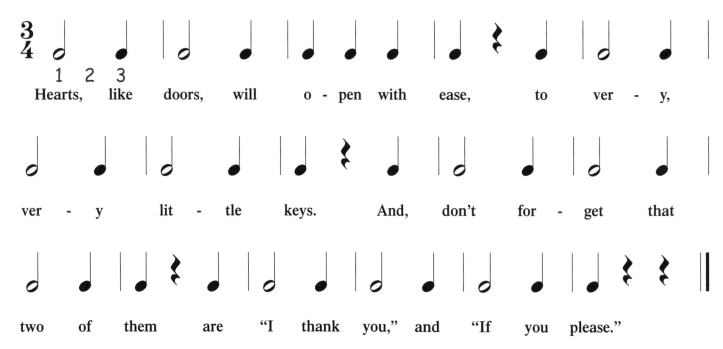

FJH2058

At the Horse Race

Time Yourself! Look at a clock!

- Write the letter names of the notes.
- Draw an X on the nearest guide note to help you.
- Then play the intervals on the piano.

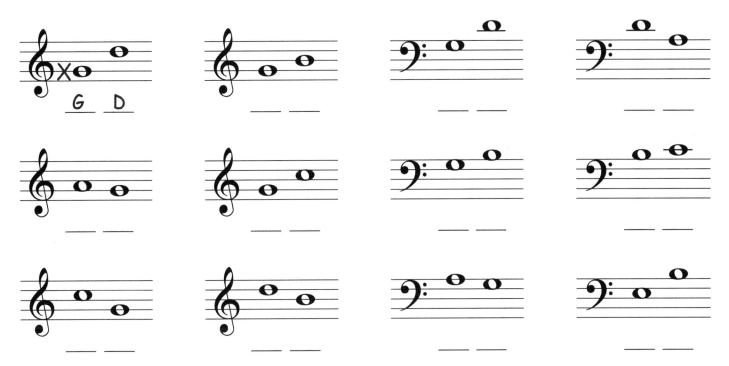

G D

- How long did it take you to finish?
  ____ Minutes _____ Seconds

Time to Compose:

- Make up a piece in G Position.
- Will the piece have 𝄽's? *staccato* notes? slurs?
- Choose a fairy tale for your title: *Cinderella, Beauty and the Beast, Rapunzel.*

My title:

_____

★ Practice your piece as many times as it takes to completely remember it!

23

It's Matching Time

Draw a line from the left to the correct answer on the right.

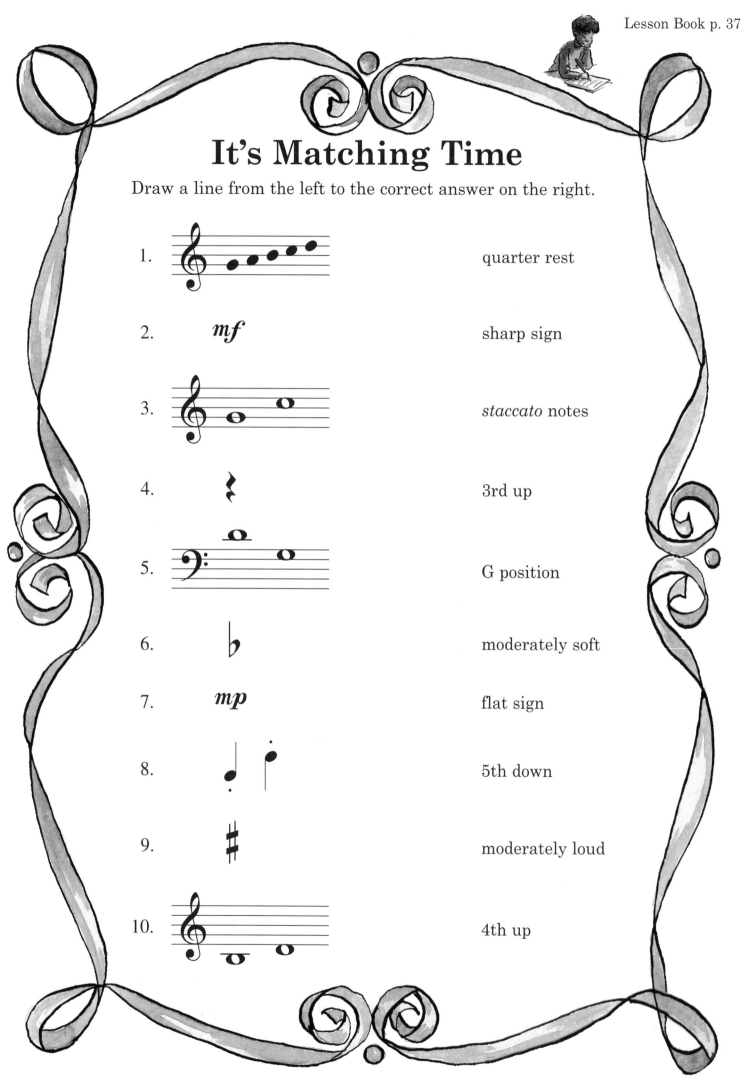

1.   quarter rest

2.   *mf*   sharp sign

3.   *staccato* notes

4.   3rd up

5.   G position

6.   moderately soft

7.   *mp*   flat sign

8.   5th down

9.   moderately loud

10.   4th up

FJH2058

Ear Training:

- Your teacher will play one pattern, a or b.
- Point to and then circle the one you hear.

1a.    1b.

2a.    2b.

3a.    3b.

Parrot Play:

- Your teacher will play melodic intervals.
- Can you **sing** the intervals?
- Can you **play** them back?

2nd

3rd

4th

5th

Now close your eyes. Your teacher will play the intervals above in any order. Write 2nd, 3rd, 4th, or 5th below.

1. _____   2. _____   3. _____   4. _____   5. _____

Half - and Whole - Rests

The half rest sits
on the 3rd line:

A half rest *always*
gets 2 beats.

The whole rest hangs
from the 4th line:
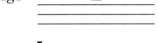

In $\frac{4}{4}$ ━ = 4 beats

In $\frac{3}{4}$ ━ = 3 beats

Draw 2 half rests:

Draw 2 whole rests:

- Write the counting under the notes.
- Tap and count aloud.
- Then play them.

Andante

mf *mp*

Adagio

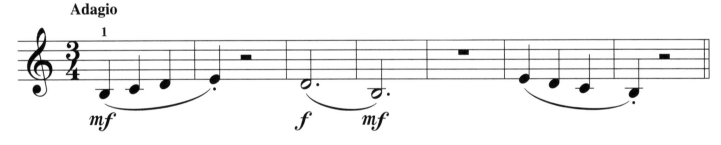

mf *f* *mf*

Time to Compose:

- Make up a piece using ━ and ━ .
- Use G Position.
- Will the piece be *p*, *mp*, *mf*, or *f*?

Some ideas: driving a car, on a bus, on an elevator.

My title:

_____

★ Practice your piece as many times as
  it takes to completely remember it!

When you practice your
piece, be sure to count!

FJH2058

Review of Rhythm

1. Draw bar lines and add a repeat sign at the end.
Then play, counting aloud.

2. For the rhymes below:
- Write the counts under the notes.
- Clap and count aloud (whisper the rests!)
- Tap and say the words.
- Add the time signatures.

Jack, Be Nimble

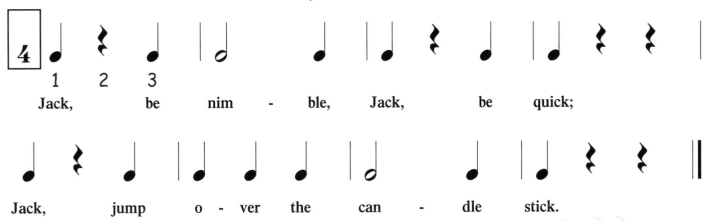

1   2   3

Jack,   be   nim - ble,   Jack,   be   quick;

Jack,   jump   o - ver   the   can - dle   stick.

Yummy Dumpling

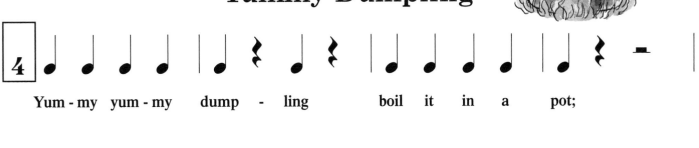

Yum - my yum - my   dump - ling   boil   it   in   a   pot;

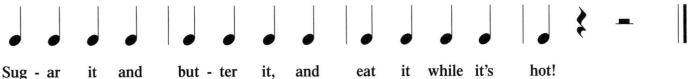

Sug - ar   it   and   but - ter   it,   and   eat   it   while   it's   hot!

Help the Knight Find His Horse!

• Draw a line from the knight to every correct answer.
  The correct path will lead you to his horse!

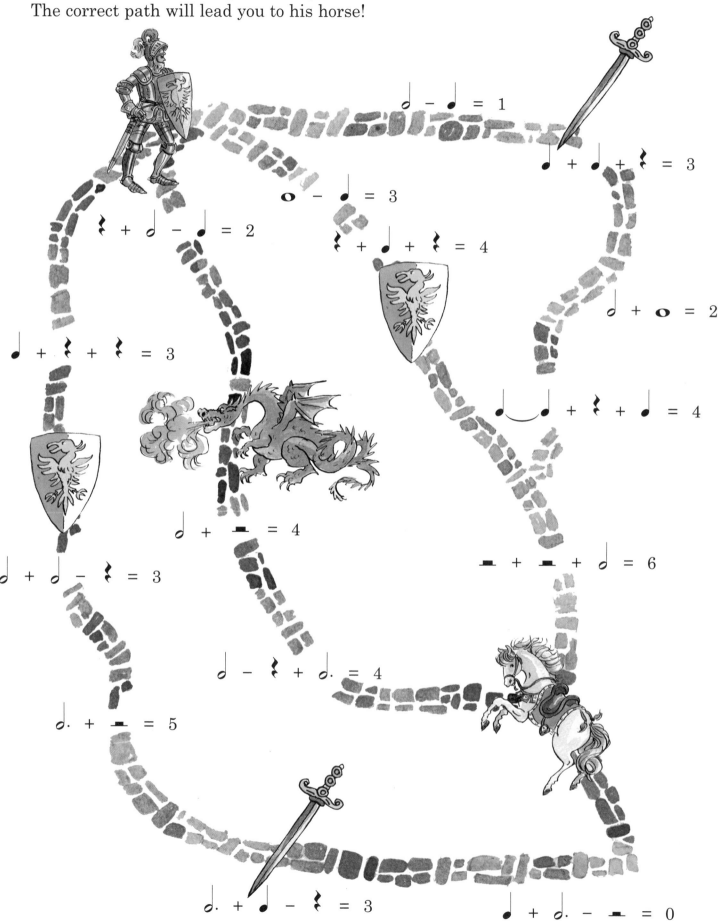

Ear Training:

- Which pattern do you hear, a or b?
  Circle it.

1a.

1b.

2a.

2b.

Follow the Leader:

- Listen to your teacher clap a rhythm.
- Can you clap it back?

For teacher use:
(Use any of these rhythms or others you might like!)

1.

2.

3.

Parrot Play:

- Without looking at the music, listen and watch your teacher play some **harmonic** intervals.
- Can you play them back?

1.

2.

3.

4.

5.

6.

Lesson Book p. 42

FACE in the Treble Clef

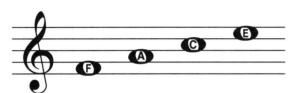

Learn the space notes in the 𝄞 clef by using the word "FACE."

1. Name each note. Then draw lines from the notes to the correct keys on the keyboard below.

_____ _____ _____ _____

2. Which space notes are the faces on? Fill in the correct answers. Then find and play the notes (faces!) on the piano.

_____ _____ _____ _____

3. Write the names of the notes and the intervals. Then play them.

F C
5th up

_____ _____
_____

_____ _____
_____

_____ _____
_____

Treble C Position

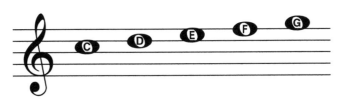

Big Boy the cat has placed a muddy paw print on every Treble C!
- Use this C as your guide note and fill in the name of the notes.

___ ___ ___ ___

___ ___ ___ ___

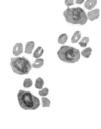

- Draw the missing notes.
- Then name both notes.
- Play the intervals on the piano.

Up a 3rd   Up a 4th   Down a 3rd   Down a 3rd
C E
___ ___   ___ ___   ___ ___   ___ ___

Up a 4th   Down a 2nd   Down a 3rd   Up a 2nd

___ ___   ___ ___   ___ ___   ___ ___

Cobbler, Cobbler

- Fill in the names of the notes to complete the story.

- Remember the guide notes:

 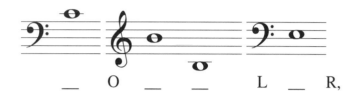

_ O _ _ L _ R,   _ O _ _ L R,

 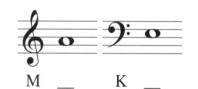

M _ N _ MY   SHO_,   M _ K _   IT

LOOK   LIK_   IT'S   _ R _ N _   N _ W.

  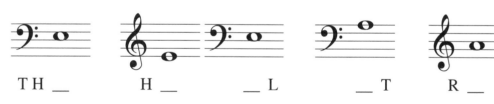 

STIT_H   TH _   H _   _ L   _ T   R _ P I _

 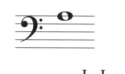 

P _   _ _,   _ L L   I N _   _ _

 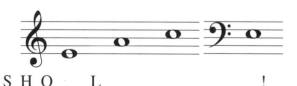

IS   _   SHO _ L _ _   _!

FJH2058

It's Matching Time

Draw a line from the left to the correct answer on the right.

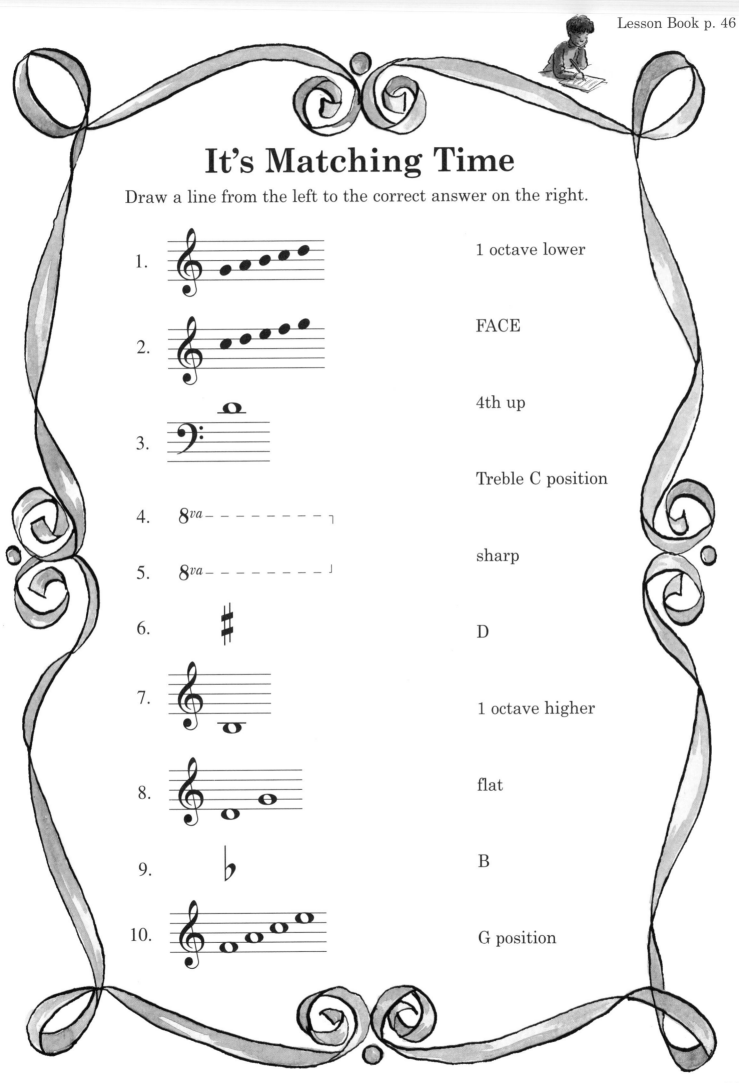

1.   1 octave lower

2.   FACE

3.   4th up

                                      Treble C position

4. *8va* – – – – – – – – ⌐

5. *8va* – – – – – – – – ⌐   sharp

6. ♯   D

7.   1 octave higher

8.   flat

9. ♭   B

10.   G position

Ear Training:

- Your teacher will play some intervals. Listen carefully!

- Write 2nd, 3rd, or 5th.

1. _____ 2._____ 3._____

4. _____ 5._____ 6._____

For teacher use: (To be played in any order.)

Follow the Leader:

- Listen to your teacher clap a rhythm.
- Can you clap it back?

For teacher use:
(Use any of these rhythms or others you might like!)

Parrot Play:

- Your teacher will play one example from each set.
- Can you play it back? (Watch and listen carefully!)
- Circle the one you hear.

(FACE)

(Treble C Position)

FJH2058

UNIT 8

Musical Form

A piece can have different sections:
   A is the first musical idea.
   A^1 is slightly changed from A.
   B is the second musical idea.

• Label the following pictures either AA^1, AB, or ABA. (Hint: the penguin is A.)

_____   _____

_____

Rhythm Review

• In each example below, place an X through the measure that is NOT correct.

• Correct them by drawing in the correct beats. Then, tap and count aloud.

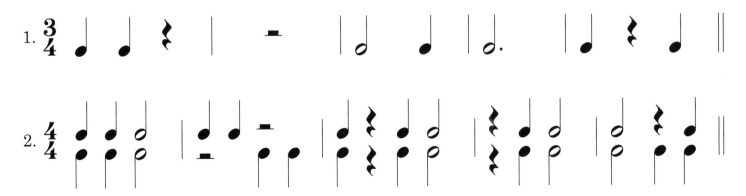

Note and Interval Review

- Label the intervals and write the note names.
- Find and play them on the piano.

3rd up

C E

_____ _____ _____

___ ___   ___ ___   ___ ___   ___ ___

___ ___   ___ ___   ___ ___   ___ ___

♯ and ♭ Review

- Write the name of the notes.
- Play them on the piano.

Db   _____   _____   _____

   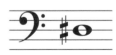

___   ___   ___   ___

FJH2058

Time to Compose:

- Make up a piece in ABA form.
- Place harmonic intervals in the L.H. in one of the sections.
- Imagine two different animals—one for the A section, the other for the B section.

My title:

_____

★ Practice your piece as many times as it takes to completely remember it!

Parrot Play:

- Your teacher will play *Row, Row, Row Your Boat*.
- Sing it together. Can you move with the rhythm?
- What is the form? AA¹, AB, ABA, (circle one.)
- Can you play it back **by ear**?

Row, Row, Row Your Boat

Traditional Round

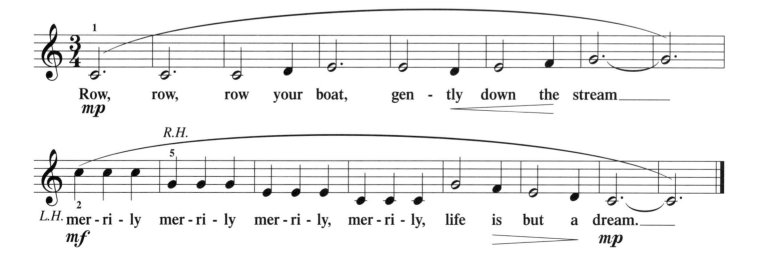

UNIT 9

Half and Whole Steps

HALF STEPS

Beethoven   Papa Haydn

From one key to the very next
key (white or black) is a half step.

WHOLE STEPS

Mozart   Chopin   Brahms

2 half steps = 1 whole step
1 key is always skipped in a whole step (X)

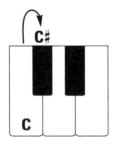

1. Place an X through the keyboards that are **not** half steps.

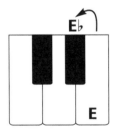
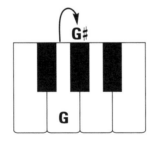

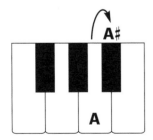
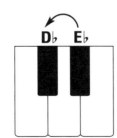
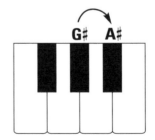
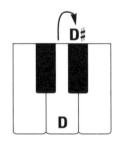

· Then play the half steps.

FJH2058

2. Place an X through the keyboards that are **not** whole steps.

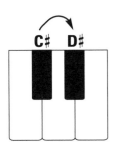 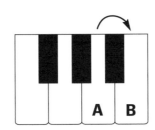 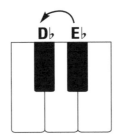 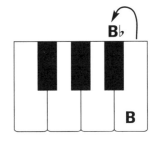

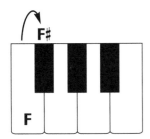  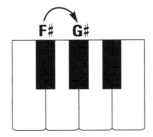 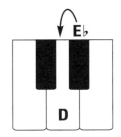

• Then play the whole steps.

3. Circle all of the half steps.
Find and play them on the piano.

Circle all of the whole steps.
Find and play them on the piano.

Ear Training:

- Do you hear half or whole steps?
- Write "H" or "W" on each line.

1. _____ 2. _____ 3. _____

4. _____ 5. _____ 6. _____

For teacher use:

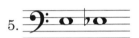

Follow the Leader:

- Point to the rhythm you hear your teacher tap, a or b.
- Then tap it back, counting aloud!

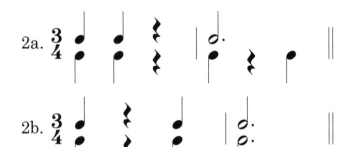

Parrot Play:

- Listen to your teacher play different patterns in D Position. Without looking at the music, can you play each pattern back?

For teacher use:

Tonic and Dominant

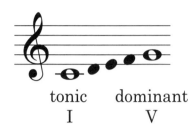

tonic   dominant
I   V

Tonic and dominant are
two important notes.

I   V

The first note of the five-finger pattern is *always* called the **tonic**.

The fifth note of the five-finger pattern is *always* called the **dominant**.

The **tonic** and **dominant** are always a 5th apart.

1. Write the dominant note in each example below.
Then play the examples.

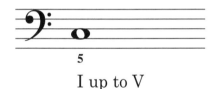

5

I up to V

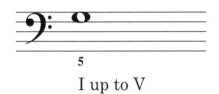

5

I up to V

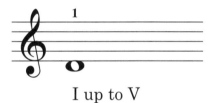

1

I up to V

2. The dominant note wants to return to the tonic.
Write the tonic note in each example.
Then play the examples.

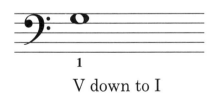

1

V down to I

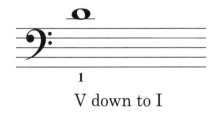

1

V down to I

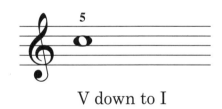

5

V down to I

3. Circle the examples that show I-V-I.

The Chicken Laid an Egg

Music based on *Go Tell Aunt Rhody*
Arrangement and new lyrics by Helen Marlais

- Write in the missing I and V notes in the L.H.
- Then play the piece.

(C position)

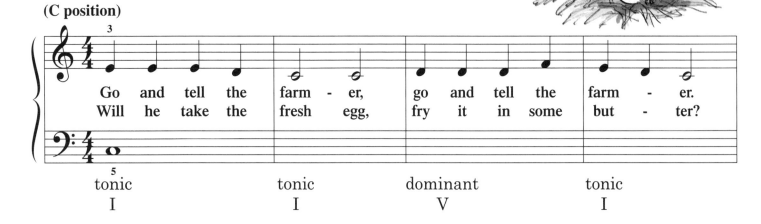

Go and tell the farm - er, go and tell the farm - er.
Will he take the fresh egg, fry it in some but - ter?

tonic   tonic   dominant   tonic
I   I   V   I

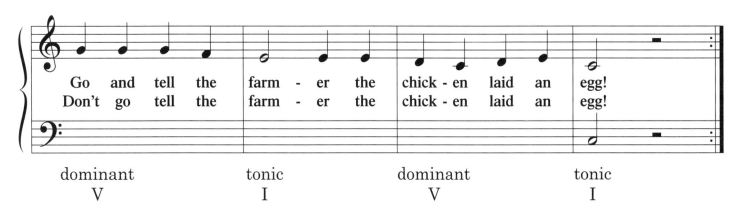

Go and tell the farm - er the chick - en laid an egg!
Don't go tell the farm - er the chick - en laid an egg!

dominant   tonic   dominant   tonic
V   I   V   I

> **Bonus!** Can you play this piece in G position?
> You are **transposing**.

Time to Compose:

Make up a piece in C, G, or D five-finger position.
- Place the I and V notes in the L.H. on every downbeat (1st beat of every measure).
- If you use fingers 1, 3, 5 in the R.H. melody, then use a I note in the L.H.
- If you use fingers 2, 4, 5 in the R.H. melody, then use a V note in the L.H.

Let your ear be your guide!

My title: _____

        FJH2058

Tonic and Dominant Notes

Ear Training:

- Listen to your teacher play tonic and dominant. Sing or say "1 - 5 - 1!" for each pattern.

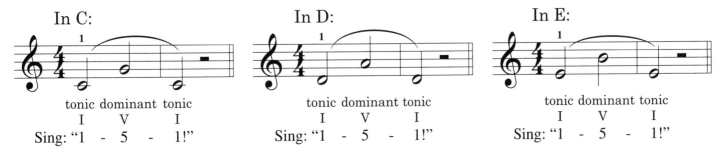

In C:

tonic dominant tonic
I   V   I
Sing: "1 - 5 - 1!"

In D:

tonic dominant tonic
I   V   I
Sing: "1 - 5 - 1!"

In E:

tonic dominant tonic
I   V   I
Sing: "1 - 5 - 1!"

- Your teacher will play melodic intervals, a or b.
- Circle the one that is the tonic - dominant - tonic.

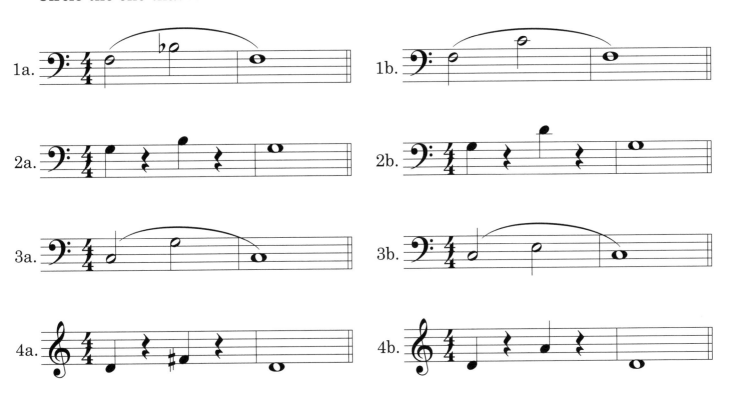

1a.   1b.

2a.   2b.

3a.   3b.

4a.   4b.

- Do not look at the keyboard for this activity!
- Your teacher will play tonic-dominant-tonic (I - V - I) notes.
- Then you will hear EITHER tonic or dominant. Tell your teacher what you hear!

Ex:
First, teacher plays:

(Teacher may play I and V notes
in a variety of different keys.)

Then, teacher plays:

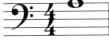

Student says: dominant

Bass G Position

- Write the names of the notes. Then play the example.

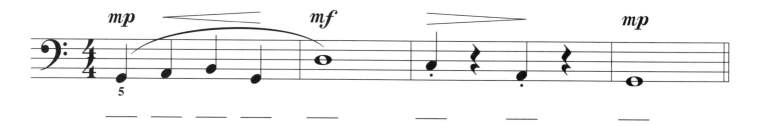

- Circle every Bass G. Then play the example.

- Circle the **melodic** intervals that use Bass G.

- Circle the **harmonic** intervals that use Bass G.

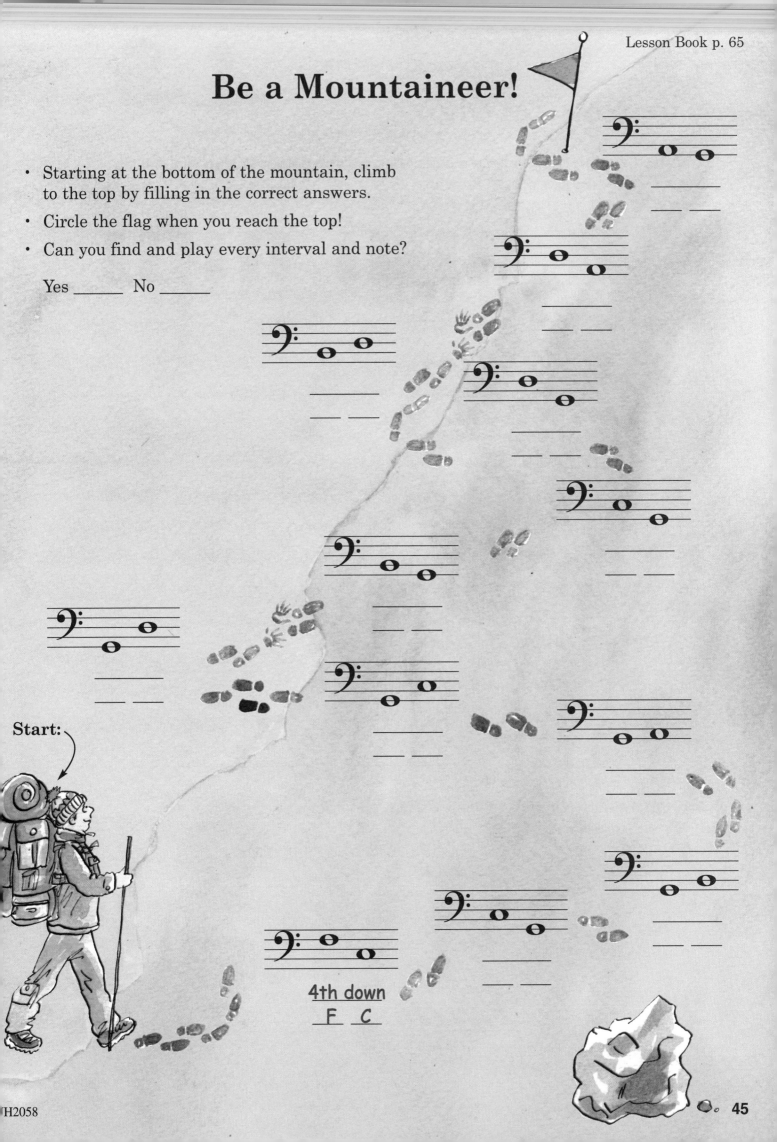

Be a Mountaineer!

- Starting at the bottom of the mountain, climb to the top by filling in the correct answers.
- Circle the flag when you reach the top!
- Can you find and play every interval and note?

Yes _____ No _____

Start:

4th down
F C

H2058

The Natural Sign ♮

A natural sign in front of a note **cancels** a sharp or a flat within the measure.
Naturals are **always** played on white keys.

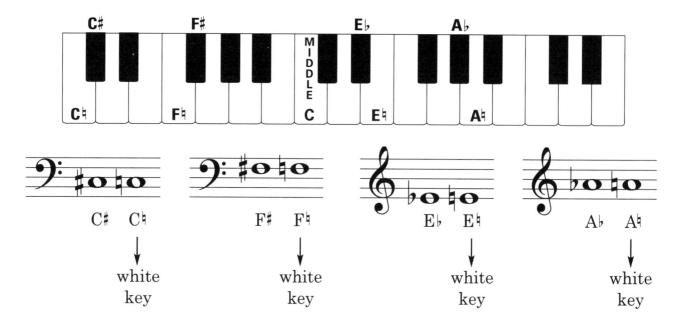

1. Trace the ♮ signs.

Draw 1st:

Draw 2nd:

Now, draw 4 of your own.

2. Write the names of the notes. Then play them.

G♯   G♮

3. Add a natural before each note. The **center** of the ♮ is **always** on the same line or space as the note head.

Then write the names of the notes.

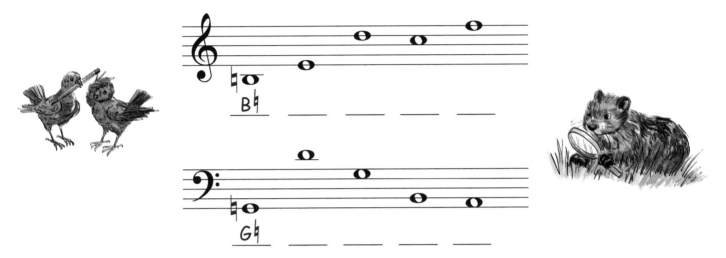

4. Write the names of the notes. Then play them.

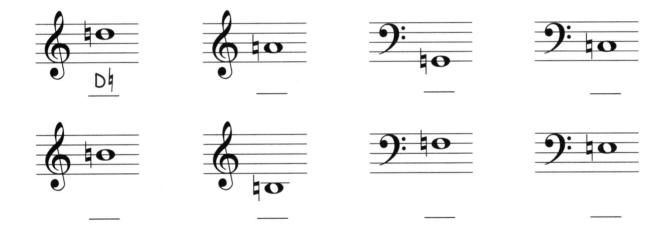

5. Write the names of the notes. Add the time signature and then play the example.

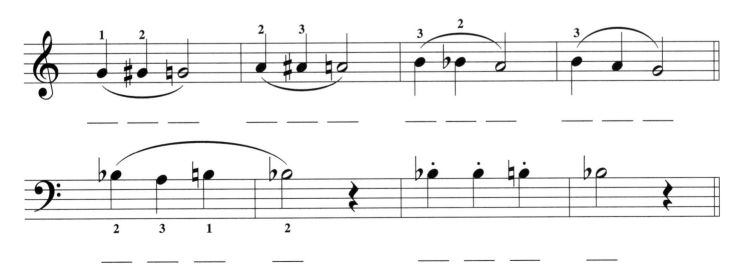

FH2058

47

Review of Sharp (♯), Flat (♭), and Natural (♮) Signs

Ear Training:

- Circle the pattern you hear, a or b.

1a.  1b.

2a. 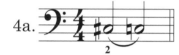 2b.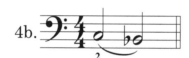

3a. 3b.

4a. 4b.

Ear Training:

Follow the Leader:

- Listen to your teacher clap a rhythm.
- Can you clap it back?

For teacher use: (To be clapped in any order.)

1.

2.

3.

4.

- Your teacher will play some intervals. Listen carefully!
- Write 2nd, 3rd, 4th, or 5th.

1. _____   2. _____   3. _____

4. _____   5. _____   6. _____

For teacher use: (To be played in any order.)

1.    2.    3.

4.    5.    6.

FJH20

Upbeats

| An upbeat is one or more notes that come before the first full measure. | Notice that the first note (the upbeat) and the two beats in the last measure equal 1 complete measure! |

1. Add the missing bar lines and the time signature. Then tap and say the words.

A Moose Named Bruce

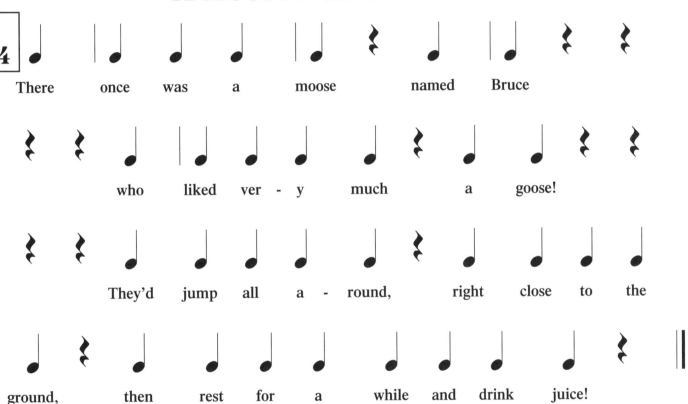

There once was a moose named Bruce

who liked ver - y much a goose!

They'd jump all a - round, right close to the

ground, then rest for a while and drink juice!

2. Place an X through the measures that have too many beats. Correct them by drawing in the correct beats. Then clap and count aloud!

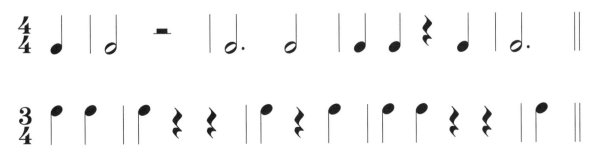

My Bonnie Lies Over the Ocean

Traditional Scottish Folk Song

- Write the counting under the notes.
- Tap and count aloud.
- Tap and say the words.

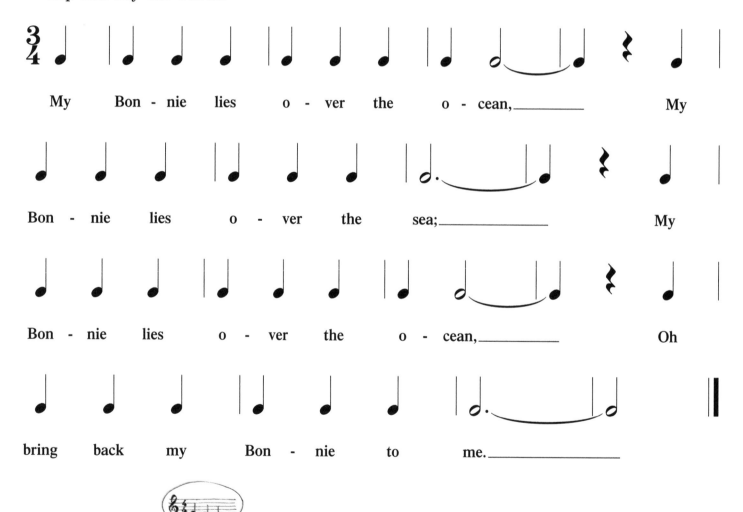

My Bon - nie lies o - ver the o - cean,_____ My

Bon - nie lies o - ver the sea;_____ My

Bon - nie lies o - ver the o - cean,_____ Oh

bring back my Bon - nie to me._____

Time to Compose:

Make up a piece using an upbeat.

- Will it be in $\frac{3}{4}$ or $\frac{4}{4}$?
- Will it have ◁—— and ——▷ ?
- Use the C, G, or D five-finger position.

My title:

_____

★ Keep it short so you'll remember it!

FJH20

Ear Training:

- Listen to two patterns. Watch and count carefully. Circle the one you hear, a or b.

1a.    1b.

2a.    2b.

Parrot Play:

- Your teacher will play *The Farmer in the Dell*.
- Sing it together. Clap it together.
- Then play the first phrase by ear.
- With practice, you will be able to play the entire piece!

The Farmer in the Dell

Traditional Folk Song

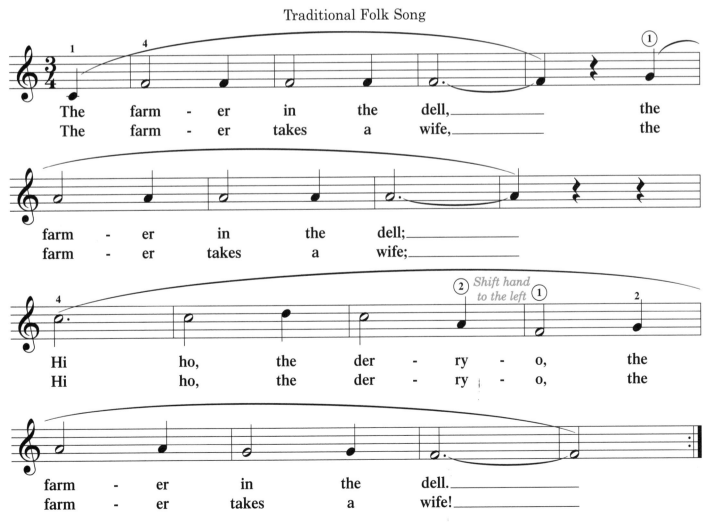

Accents

Accents show when a note is played louder than the other notes around it.

1. Using 𝄽, add the missing rests below.
Write the counting under the notes.
Clap and count aloud (whisper the rests!)
Then tap and say the words.

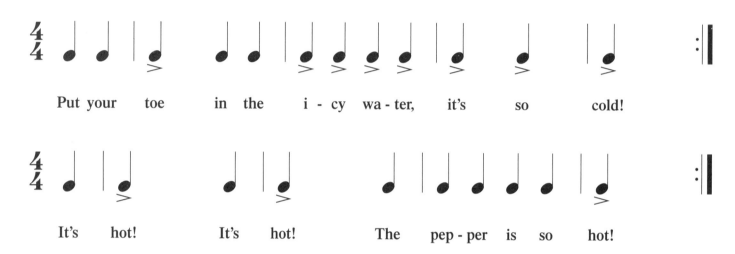

Put your toe in the i - cy wa - ter, it's so cold!

It's hot! It's hot! The pep - per is so hot!

2. Add the missing time signature.
Draw an accent mark on every downbeat (first beat).
Clap and count aloud.
Tap and say the words.

Hoo - ray! Hoo - ray! It's sum - mer - time a - gain! I'll

fish and swim and climb big trees and stay up late 'til ten!

It's Matching Time

Draw a line from the left to the correct answer on the right.

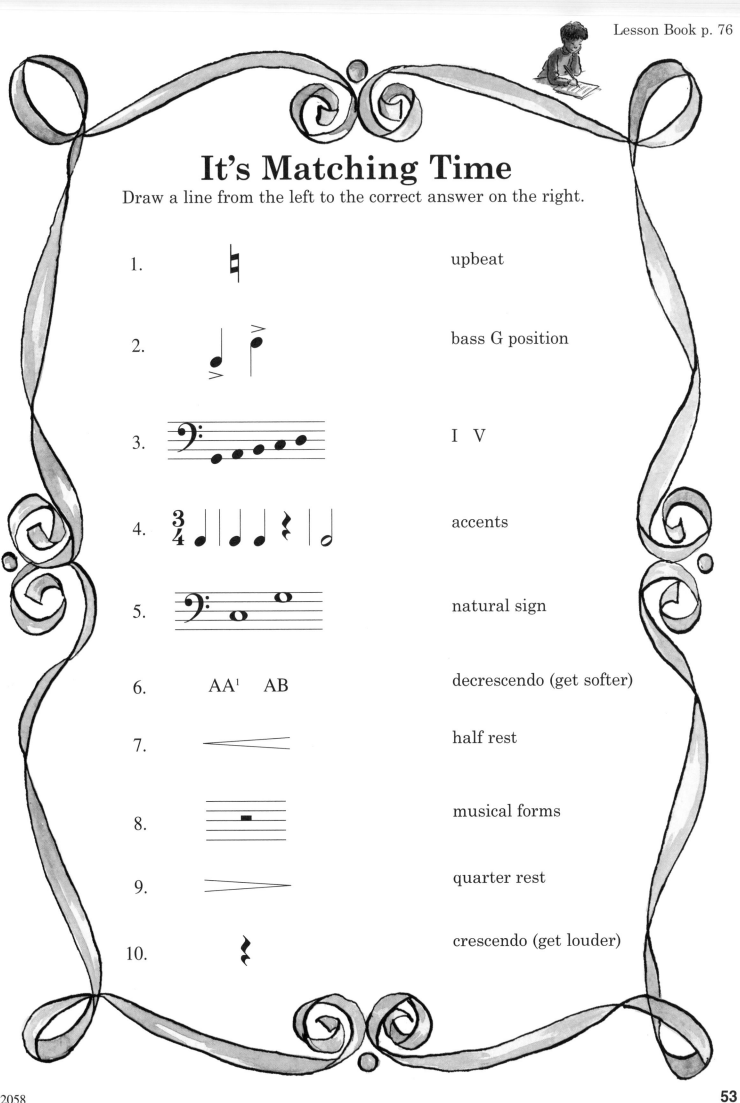

1.   upbeat

2.   bass G position

3.   I   V

4.   accents

5.   natural sign

6.   AA¹   AB   decrescendo (get softer)

7.   half rest

8.   musical forms

9.   quarter rest

10.   crescendo (get louder)

Be a Star!

- Draw a line from each star to the correct names of the notes in the grass.

FJH2

Hall of Fame—Which Composer Is It?

- You have learned about famous composers in your *Lesson and Technique Book* and *Recital Book*.
- Draw a line from the composer to the fact that matches below.

Haydn

Mozart

Beethoven

Chopin

Brahms

Schumann

This composer wrote *Ode to Joy*. (page 46 Lesson)

This composer wrote symphonies for the people of London, England. (page 22 Lesson)

This composer grew up in Poland but spent most of his life in Paris, France. (page 28 Lesson)

This composer from Germany wrote *Hungarian Dance No. 5*. (page 49 Lesson)

This composer was married to a pianist named Clara. (page 73 Recital)

This composer was born in Austria and played for kings and queens in Europe. (page 62 Lesson)

Certificate of Achievement

_____

Student

has completed

Helen Marlais'
Succeeding at the Piano®

Theory and Activity Book

GRADE 1

You are now ready for

GRADE 2A

_____   _____

Date   Teacher's Signature

THE
F·J·H
MUSIC
COMPANY
INC.

Frank J. Hackinson